Humpty Dumpty Finances

Putting the Pieces Back Together Again

Stephon Lee

> To buy books in quantity (500 or more) for corporate use or incentives call 770-778-0430 or email stephonlee@budgetyourdream.com.

Humpty Dumpty Finances ™
Copyright © 2013 by Assets Diversified Investments, Inc.

ISBN 978-0-578-12015-7

ALL RIGHTS RESERVED.
No part of this book may be reproduced or transmitted in any form by any means, electronic or mechanical, including photocopying and recording, or by any information storage and retrieval system, except as may be expressly permitted in writing from the publisher.

First Edition
Library of Congress Cataloging-in-Publication Data has been applied for.

Printed in the United States of America

Humpty Dumpty Finances is a trademark of Assets Diversified Investments, Inc.

To the millions who are
experiencing or have experienced financial
difficulties, you are not alone.

At times, you may feel or have felt like
Humpty Dumpty.

I hope that this book
will inspire you to avoid the Humpty Dumpty
experience.

And for those who have fallen,
I hope this book will help you to put your finances
back together again.

TABLE OF CONTENTS

Forward	....	1
Chapter 1	Make the Decision	3
Chapter 2	Surround Yourself with a Capable Team ..	17
Chapter 3	Ask for Help – Don't Wait Too Late	23
Chapter 4	Don't Live Above Your Means	31
Chapter 5	Secure Your Position	39
Chapter 6	Create a Safety Net	63
Chapter 7	Simplify Your Finances	71
Chapter 8	Relieve the Pain	79
Chapter 9	Having Adequate Income	85
Chapter 10	Take Action and Budget	91
Chapter 11	Seven Points to Remember	103
Chapter 12	Tools to Get Started	105
	◊ Starting Day 1	109
	◊ Starting Day 8	115
	◊ Starting Day 15	121
	◊ Starting Day 22	127
	◊ Budget Months 1, 2 and 3	133
Acknowledgements	....	141
About the Author	....	143

FOREWORD

Much like Humpty Dumpty in the well known children's nursery rhyme, many people have fallen and their finances are shattered.

Humpty Dumpty Finances is a book that will help many people learn how to avoid a financial fall. The book will motivate millions in taking the first step towards fixing their broken finances.

It will equip and empower generations to come with financial knowledge, sound financial principles and insight to better financial management.

Humpty Dumpty Finances is a must read for the individual or family who wants to better manage their finances or is experiencing a tough financial struggle whether caused by job loss, foreclosure, illness, divorce, business failure or bad financial decisions.

This book contains the answers for those seeking how to get well and how to break the grip of financial despair.

Humpty Dumpty Finances will stimulate each reader into making a positive lifestyle change. Included in the book are tools, worksheets and tips that are useful to help control spending, save money and put the broken pieces back together.

Chapter 1

MAKE THE DECISION

I Can and I Will

Many of us know this nursery rhyme from our childhood, "Humpty Dumpty sat on the wall and Humpty had a great fall. All the king's horses and all the king's men could not put Humpty back together again."

Much like Humpty Dumpty, many have experienced some type of a fall or perhaps feel like they are about to lose control of their finances.

What should a person do when he or she has reached an all time low in his or her finances? The bills are overdue, going to the mail box is a stressful experience, collection notices are received daily, there are more bills than money and there seems to be nothing else to cut from the budget. Furthermore, finding a higher paying job is hard to do and starting a business requires money that the person does not have. Borrowing money is not an option because the person's credit has been destroyed by juggling money to pay bills.

Difficult financial and economic conditions along with poor financial management have led to a fall leaving the finances of many people in ruin. Many are frustrated, distressed and do not know what to do or where to start. In their pain, they feel weak and hopeless. They see their financial situation as a problem that's too hard to resolve and the possibility of recovery too far-away.

A lot like Humpty, many people were also sitting comfortably and unaware of imminent danger until they incurred a fall leaving their lives and finances devastated.

How could a tragedy paramount to Humpty's fall happen over and over again in so many people lives today? For many, the fall is caused by a job loss, personal and family illnesses, divorce, business failure or the implosion caused by excessive debt and overspending.

The results of these calamities are lives turned upside

down, credit destroyed, massive and mounting debt, along with low and decreasing savings. Even worst, some of these individuals will have to manage their financial challenges with less household income.

For those who has fallen deep into financial trouble, it seems as though a financial war has been declared. Many are bombarded daily with bill collectors demanding payment and payment arrangements. For some this reality is too much to bear.

Unfortunately, too many give up fighting for a positive change in their financial condition; instead, they accept it as a way of life. Until these challenges are faced and resolved, individuals become trapped by mounting debt, less income, lower savings and a poorer standard of living.

How does a person recover from this type of financial nightmare? Just like anyone caught in a trap with no foreseeable way out, the person must decide to either break out of the trap or do nothing and accept the painful existence.

In a desperate and emotional situation, logic and sound reasoning will still need to prevail. In order for a person

to begin the recovery process, the person must be willing to make a sincere commitment to fix the problem.
.

"I can and I will" attitude and commitment will be the starting point to recovery. Financial success will begin and be achieved by a relentless commitment to putting the broken pieces back together.

The "I can and I will" attitude and commitment may seem overly simple but it is crucial and essential to sustaining the long-term and painstaking effort that is usually required to rebuild and grow a solid financial future.

Humpty Dumpty gave up. The result of giving up is a big mess. Giving up leaves pieces and clutter scattered everywhere. When one quits the story ends with a broken life and an unfilled purpose.

"Humpty Dumpty Finances" is when our finances are broken and we give up hope and cease the unrelenting determination and persistent effort necessary to put the pieces back together again.

Maybe there are those we know who have fallen into excessive debt, suffered job losses, or major financial defeats and they have lost confidence and are on the verge of giving up.

Perhaps a family member, friend or coworker has fallen and now has given up and no longer tries to put his or her life back together. He or she has quit and is tired because the road to recovery seems too hard, too great, and too long.

In the darkest hour the message is the same to us all. Don't quit. Keep the determination to succeed. Throughout history those who had the resolve to achieve success overcame a great deal of failures. For example, a corporation by the name of WD-40 Company, Inc. which is well known today, failed 39 times before it was able to get its formula right. The company on its 40th attempt was able to correctly create a line of rust-prevention solvents and degreasers. The company name stands for Water Displacement perfected on the 40th attempt. If the company had quit before the 40th attempt the knowledge gained from the previous attempts would have been a loss. Instead each of the 39 failures was a learning opportunity for greatness.

Another example is our 16th President, Abraham Lincoln.

Before becoming President, Abraham Lincoln experienced business failure and high debts. As a captain in the military he was discharged and reenlisted as a private. In his political career he faced defeat. Yet in all the hard setbacks, Abraham Lincoln prevailed as one of the greatest American presidents. Abraham Lincoln did not quit. He maintained the tenacity and progressed to accomplish greatness.

There are many examples of people overcoming difficulties and attaining high achievements. Just to name a few more entrepreneurs like Henry Ford of the Ford Company, R. H. Macy of Macy's Department Stores, Soichiro Honda of the Honda Corporation, Bill Gates of Microsoft Corporation and Walt Disney of The Walt Disney Company faced major setbacks and some of them experienced bankruptcy numerous times before becoming a large success.

Somewhere along the way Humpty Dumpty lost hope and determination much like a lot of people when faced with a major setback.

Who knows why Humpty gave up? Maybe Humpty had fallen before and he knew the difficulty of rebuilding.

Perhaps, just the mere thought of the long and difficult journey to recovery was too much for Humpty.

It is easy to take Humpty Dumpty's attitude and mindset when facing a difficult situation. Our lives can become much like the Humpty Dumpty who thought that he could not be put back together again. Regardless how tough the challenge may be to put the pieces back together again, one should not lose hope.

The reality is that most likely the road to financial recovery will be long and hard. The good news is that the sooner you get started the sooner you can finish.

Putting your finances back together requires taking action and following a sound financial plan. Sacrifices are necessary to achieve your financial goals. Those having an "I can and I will" attitude are more likely to succeed.

Below is a "Personal Journal." You can take a moment and write a personal note or letter expressing your desire, decision, and commitment to making a positive financial change.

Your commitment can be expressed to yourself, family member, friend, or in a prayer to God.

The "Personal Journal" will be a good reminder of your decision, confidence and commitment to a positive change towards better financial management.

The key is not to delay any longer. Begin now by making a sincere decision and commitment to achieve your goals.

Personal Journal

I am writing in my journal today to express my desires, decisions, confidence and commitment to make the necessary changes required to reach my financial goals.

"I can" and "I will" take action, make the financial sacrifices and not quit. Today I am making a commitment to change for the better.

Dear: _____

Here are my words to express my thoughts, desires, decisions, confidence and commitment to positive change.

_____
_____
_____
_____
_____
_____

Signed by: _____

Date: _____

In the remaining parts of this chapter, we will briefly present and discuss two final points. The first will be related to the need to identify the root causes of finance problems or concerns. The second and final point of this chapter will be related to behavior changes required for better financial management.

After a person makes a firm decision and commitment to fix or improve his or her financial situation, the person should begin to identify the root cause of the financial concern.

The key to fixing the problem is to know and understand what caused or is causing the financial problem. For example, if a boat has a leak in it and the leak is not fixed, the boat may float a while but eventually the boat will sink unless the leak is fixed.

If a person has a leak in his or her finances that causes a serious problem or threat to his or her financial future, the specific leak will need to be identified and fixed. If not, that person sooner or later could find himself or herself financially under water struggling for survival. The leak will need to be fixed in order to protect the wellness of the person's finances.

There are various root causes of financial problems. One example is a lack of planning or financial vision. Lack of planning will lead to serious financial problems. Looking ahead and planning for unexpected and possibly dangerous situations are essential to good financial management.

Let's return to Humpty Dumpty. Perhaps, Humpty had a vision problem. Humpty may have failed to look ahead and properly plan his steps. Had he looked ahead and planned for potentially slippery conditions, he may have avoided taking steps that put him at risk of falling.

At the end of this chapter is a simple form titled, "Root Causes of Financial Hardship or Concerns". This form can be used to begin the process of identifying the root causes of a person's financial problems or concerns.

A final point in this chapter is that one of the biggest challenges most will face is overcoming their own resistance to make the behavior changes required to rebuild or better manage their finances for long-term success.

If financial success is to be achieved, one must be self disciplined and motivated to make the required changes. In most cases, change is not easy but necessary. The good news is financial success is achievable when a person takes ownership, control and responsibility for the outcome.

Below are examples of behavior changes a person can take to improve his or her finances. This subject will be explored in more details in Chapter 10, "Take Action and Budget." Most behavior changes will require an adjustment in a person's spending, planning and time management.

Changing behavior includes:
- ✓ making a decision and commitment to improve
- ✓ creating a budget
- ✓ lowering household expenses
- ✓ eliminating purchases that are not necessary
- ✓ avoiding purchases that are not affordable
- ✓ paying bills as timely as possible to reduce late fees
- ✓ monitoring your expenditures
- ✓ adjusting your spending plan as needed

- ✓ reducing debt
- ✓ lowering interest costs
- ✓ refinancing debt
- ✓ negotiating debt settlements
- ✓ saving for unexpected expenses and emergencies
- ✓ seeking financial and legal professional help when necessary

Other behavior changes may include:

- ✓ working longer hours
- ✓ changing jobs and careers
- ✓ taking on an additional job to supplement your income
- ✓ increasing your job skills, training, educational background, and aptitude necessary to increase your earnings potential

If you have not completed the "Personal Journal" on page 11 and the "Root Causes of Hardship and Concerns" form on the following page, you may want to take a moment and do so at this time.

Root Causes of Financial Hardship or Concerns

Check the boxes below that best indicate the root causes of your financial hardship or concerns.

- ☐ Job Loss/Unemployed/Lack of Income
- ☐ Lack of Budgeting
- ☐ Business Failure
- ☐ Poor Money Management
- ☐ Too Much Debt
- ☐ Over Spending
- ☐ Lack of Financial Planning
- ☐ Lack of Savings (less than 6 months of living expenses)
- ☐ Recent Divorce
- ☐ Personal or Family Illness

List some of the things you plan to do to improve your finances.

_____
_____
_____
_____
_____

Chapter 2

Surround Yourself with a Capable Team

"All the king's horses and all the king's men could not put Humpty back together again."

When people surround themselves with those who are neither capable of giving wise advice nor able to help fix the broken pieces, the end result is "Humpty Dumpty Finances."

Having sound and wise advice is crucial to preventing a fall, as well as, recovering from a fall.

One of the best books regarding wisdom is the book of Proverbs. Proverbs stresses the importance of wise counsel.

Proverbs tells us, *"Where no counsel is the people fall: but in the multitude of counselors there is safety. Without counsel purposes are disappointed: but in the multitude of counselors they are established."*

If you cannot do it on your own, it is very important that you obtain good advice from qualified sources. Do the following to begin building your team:

- ✓ Research the qualifications of your adviser. You can begin by talking with others. Personal references are always one of the best sources of information.

- ✓ Interview your potential adviser to learn about his or her field of expertise and their level of experience.

- ✓ Ask for referrals.

- ✓ Take the opportunity to talk with previous clients.

- ✓ Review websites and other online sources for information about the adviser's services and costs.

- ✓ Ask for the required fees or compensation in writing so that you can make sure that you are not charged a fee that you do not agree with or understand. Avoid advisers that do not make the costs of their services easy and simple to be understood.

- ✓ Seek someone that you can trust. If you have second thoughts or do not trust the adviser's ability and integrity then you should avoid him or her.

There are nonprofit organizations that can provide advisers or coaches to assist with budgeting, home buying, credit counseling, debt management and other financial related matters.

Organizations can include the following:

- ✓ Consumer Credit Counseling Services - CCCS (www.nfcc.org)
- ✓ Financial Fitness Center (www.ffcenter.org)
- ✓ Home Free USA (www.homefreeusa.org)
- ✓ HUD Approved Housing Counseling Agencies (www.hud.gov) **Note**: HUD's Approved Agencies are listed under the "Resources" link
- ✓ InCharge Debt Solutions (www.incharge.org)
- ✓ National Urban League (www.nul.org)
- ✓ NACA (www.naca.com)
- ✓ NeighborWorks America (www.nw.org)
- ✓ Operation Hope (www.operationhope.org)

Most of these services do not require any out of pocket costs and if so, it is usually nominal. You should visit their websites to learn more.

Your mortgage company or bank may also be able to refer you to a qualified organization that can provide financial coaching or counseling to help you.

You should look for advisers who seek to understand your situation and the goals you wish to accomplish. If you are recovering from a job loss or foreclosure and you have large amounts of debt, you should seek an adviser who can help you with budgeting and debt management.

Your adviser should be able to provide you directions on how to best eliminate, settle, negotiate, reduce interest rates or pay your debts with a payment plan.

Ongoing budgeting is necessary to reduce debts and build savings. If you are working with an adviser, the adviser should help you to prepare a budget and show you how to find ways to further reduce your expenses.

A good adviser should help you understand the best approach to rebuilding. Your adviser should be someone you are comfortable with. As you seek out your team to help you move forward, it is important that you find a team that is also positive. Regardless of your recovery plan and financial goals, you and your advisers must be confident that your goals can be accomplished.

Family members, friends or members from your place of worship can be a good source for advice and inspiration. Whatever your source, make sure that the financial advice is sound. Those closest, if qualified, can be an excellent choice because they should have your best interest at heart and are generally more accessible.

However, it is prudent to be discerning in choosing financial advisers. Sometimes within your immediate sphere of family and friends, they are not the most capable or the best advisers to help put your finances back together or manage your finances.

As in the story of Humpty Dumpty, all the king's men and all the king's horses could not put him back together again. Perhaps Humpty Dumpty should have looked beyond the king's men to find a source that was more capable. If he had, perhaps the story would have ended differently.

Even with the best team of advisers and financial plans, recovery and financial success will not be obtained unless you take action and follow the sound advice provided.

Chapter 3

Ask for Help – Don't Wait Too Late

As we know Humpty Dumpty fell. But did Humpty ask for help as soon as he noticed that he was about to lose his grip? Maybe if Humpty had asked for help beforehand, he could have avoided the fall.

It is very important that as soon as you see that you are having trouble paying your bills that you ask for help. Don't wait. It is easier to help prevent a fall than to make major repairs after the fall has occurred.

If you are having trouble with your mortgage, don't wait until you get a foreclosure notice and have been foreclosed on to ask for help. Instead call your bank or mortgage company immediately and request help. Explain your situation and ask for help. The bank or mortgage company will determine the best solution to help prevent foreclosure and save you from falling.

There are several options that the bank or mortgage company can discuss with you. For example some of the options the bank or mortgage company may present are forbearance, repayment plan, loan modification, or short sale.

Forbearance allows you to reduce or suspend payments for a short period of time. You will be required after the forbearance period to bring your loan current. If you enter into a forbearance agreement make certain you understand the agreement.

A Repayment Plan is an agreement to resume making your regular monthly payments, plus a portion of the past due payments each month until you are caught up.

Loan modification may occur when you don't have enough money to bring your account current or you can't afford your current payment. Your lenders may be willing to change the terms of your mortgage to include changes such as changing the terms to allow you to add the missed payments to the existing loan balance, changing the interest rate, converting an adjustable rate to a fixed rate, or extending the number of years you have to repay the loan. A loan modification is usually a long-term or permanent change to the terms of the loan.

Calling your lender immediately to ask for help is the first and best option for you. A simple call for help to your bank or mortgage company may save your home from foreclosure and reduce the financial hardships that could lead to a financial fall.

It is better to call your lender and request help in private than to broadcast the problem to others when you are forced out of your home by foreclosure. This is a tragedy when a home could have been saved by a simple call to the lender asking for help.

There are the Department of Housing and Urban Development (HUD) approved housing counseling agencies that you can call to talk with if you are uncomfortable talking first with your bank or mortgage company. When reaching out for help, you must be consistent and assertive. Do not wait if someone does not call you back immediately. You should continue to call them until you receive the help you need. The bank or mortgage company is also willing to provide you with a HUD approved housing counseling agency where you can call to talk with a counselor. HUD Approved Housing Counseling Agencies provide their advice and assistance at no cost.

Most banks and mortgage companies have representatives who can immediately begin providing help and solutions to saving your home. Remember, the bank and mortgage companies do not want your home. They want to maintain a good relationship with you as the lender. They want you to keep the home.

However, if you stop making payments and do not communicate with them, they will foreclose on your home. Unless you tell them about your situation, your lender will have no other choice but to foreclose. But when you call them, you can work out a solution to save your home.

When you can afford to pay your mortgage you should make your required payments until you can work out a more affordable or desirable arrangement with your lender. To walk away from your home will leave you with other liabilities that you may not have considered. If you walk away or allow the lender to foreclose on your home, you could be held accountable for the difference in the amount owed on the home verses what the lender received from the sale of your property.

Many states give lenders the ability to seize bank deposits, cars or other assets including rental properties owned by the people who default on mortgages. The lender's loss on the property could be placed on your credit report and continually pursued by a debt collector until the balance is paid, settled or resolved in a legal way.

When you walk away from a mortgage and the property goes into foreclosure, the neighborhood is further harmed by lowering property values. Whenever possible do not walk away from your mortgage when given alternative solutions. Another consequence one needs to consider before choosing to walk away from an affordable mortgage is the negative message being sent to their family, friends, children and close associates.

Many people consider individuals who walk away from their financial obligation to be irresponsible and not trustworthy in dealing with financial matters. You should consider all factors including the negative perception and reputation that could result from you choosing to walk away from a property that you could afford to pay or have worked out other arrangements.

Do all that is within your ability to pay your mortgage and prevent foreclosures. Paying your mortgage is the financially and socially responsible thing to do. However, if your mortgage is not affordable and you cannot work out a solution with your bank or mortgage company and all parties have determined that foreclosure is unavoidable then work with your bank to seek what other options can be arranged in lieu of foreclosure.

Seek to make your transaction as smooth as possible. Talk with your lender about "Keys for Cash" program, which allows you to turn in your keys for a cash payment. The lender pays the homeowner cash to vacate the property. The cash can be very beneficial to assisting you with relocation expenses. Your lender may be participating in this program or some other similar programs.

If you are interested in being considered for "Keys for Cash" program and you are filing bankruptcy, the bankruptcy filing may disqualify you from receiving the

"Keys for Cash". When you file bankruptcy the attorney will ask whether you have any cash, tax refunds, settlement, lottery winnings or any money coming to you. If so, any funds coming to you could be seized by the courts as payment to your creditors as part of the bankruptcy.

If your home has already been foreclosed on by the lender don't wait to begin rebuilding your finances. If you need help, find a qualified adviser to assist you. This book will be useful in providing tips and insight to help you with the rebuilding process.

Regardless of the type of debt, most creditors want to work with borrowers to avoid loan defaults. If you have trouble paying your credit cards, auto or student loans, you should call your creditors to work out a payment plan. There are options your creditors may consider to help you stay current on your debts. Your creditors may be willing to reduce your interest rate, eliminate late fees, lower monthly payments or defer payments for a period of time.

Don't wait too late to communicate. Speak with your creditors as soon as you see that you are losing your grip or balance. Don't wait to fall like Humpty Dumpty. In hind sight, it would have been a lot easier to have stopped Humpty from a fall than it is to put Humpty back together again.

Be wise about money and avoid a financial fall when possible. Preventing a fall is easier than recovering from a fall. Sound financial wisdom is reducing your debt and paying the ones you have on time. If you are faced with a challenge, you should contact your creditors to work out an amicable solution to repay your debt.

Chapter 4

Don't Live Above Your Means

Living above your means will most certainly position you for a fall. When you are spending in excess of your income, you are living above your means, which will eventually lead to a fall.

Given Humpty's physical vulnerability, he should have been aware of his condition, limited his risk and avoided the activities that would have put him at risk of being severely harmed.

Like Humpty, many people today enjoy the excitement of sitting high and living financially above what is within their means. Often we buy homes and cars that we cannot afford. We take on debt, spend money and consume things that are beyond what is recommended, given our income, debt level and financial capabilities.

Generally, there are warning signs that let us know we are at risk of a fall. Many times the warning signs are obvious to detect if we take a moment to stop and take notice. A simple self-evaluation can be conducted by a few "what if" questions.

For example, Humpty Dumpty could have asked himself these simple questions. What if I slipped due to an unforeseen event? Am I prepared for a fall? Will I be able to withstand the fall? Am I able or positioned to avoid a fall? Perhaps, a simple and honest self-evaluation will prompt us to make a major change in the way we manage our lives.

Just imagine, Humpty may have become so enamored and proud of securing one of the finest walls with breathtaking scenery located in the heart of a private and exclusive community that he never considered his limited capabilities to sustain and maintain his balance on the wall.

It is understandable how Humpty could have gotten emotionally attached to such an elite and high priced wall where he would be admired by others who only wished they too could sit so high. Many of his acquaintances may have wondered how Humpty could live so high on the wall given his limited resources.

Humpty may have seen others sitting high on the wall and living in luxury. In the words of the cliché, Humpty was keeping up with the Joneses. There were other walls that may have been better suited for Humpty. Humpty thought those walls were too low, too small, and not impressive. Those walls were not in the right neighborhoods. He needed a wall that he could brag about to his friends and family. He needed a wall that would make him look like a great success.

Humpty was determined to take the wall on the hill. This wall was one of the most expensive and prominent walls in the community. This wall was very high and suited for a king. Humpty wanted his gratification now and there was no one stopping him from buying the wall that he wanted. He would no longer wait or count the risk. Humpty was no longer listening or considering sound advice.

Like many today, Humpty's main concern was satisfying

his immediate desires and enjoying a risky lifestyle without thinking about the consequences. Unfortunately, Humpty lost his balance and fell.

The higher people live beyond their income, the greater the opportunity for a financial fall. The more people spend beyond their income the harder the challenge will be, after a fall, to put the pieces back together again.

It is very important not to buy what you cannot afford. In order to help prevent overspending or making long-term debt obligations that are beyond what you can afford, create a budget to determine what is affordable.

Example 1: If you are buying a home that will cost you $1,500 per month and your monthly household gross income is $3,000 per month you are setting yourself up for a financial problem that will most likely cause you to fall. Incurring long-term debt equal to 50% of your gross monthly income is an example of living beyond your means.

Example 2: Your monthly housing cost is $1,500, with other monthly debts totaling $550. Your household monthly income, including your spouse, is $5,000 per month. You are planning to buy a second car with a monthly payment of $500 per month. If you purchase a second car, the monthly debts would total $2,550, which will exceed 50% of the gross monthly income.

As a general rule your total debt should not exceed 36% of your gross monthly income. Your mortgage payment, including principal, interest, real estate taxes, homeowner's insurance should not exceed 28% of your gross monthly income. Lenders often use these debt to income ratios as the "not to exceed percentages" when considering mortgage loan applications for approval.

Example 3: If Bob has a $45,000 gross salary his mortgage payment including taxes, insurances and any other fees should not exceed $1,050. His total monthly debt, including the mortgage payment should not exceed $1,350.

When you take on debt outside of these guidelines, you are living above your means. Living a lifestyle beyond your income leads to Humpty Dumpty Finances.

Buying a home or car is a long-term purchase. It is very easy to be lured into buying more than what you can afford. Remember the old cliché of keeping up with the Joneses is very appealing to most people as they want the biggest and best house among their peers. So when their peers buy a $400,000 house, the compelling appeal and competitive nature of people drive them to want something comparable or better.

Often people will spend money in excess of what they should or can afford simply for bragging rights and to associate with a specific group of people. However, this type of decision making can be very dangerous because the buying decision is no longer logical, but emotional.

When one's emotions take control the end result is usually buying what is not needed or more than what is affordable. In either case, poor financial management will lead to financial stress, anxiety, hardship, and eventually a financial fall.

If you are living above your means, the sooner you can come down from the high wall the better and safer you will be. Having a debt to income ratio in excess of 36% is an indication that you have climbed too high. You are stretching the limits. Begin to climb down step by step. Lower your expenses and reduce your debts.

Climbing down by lowering your expenses and debts will take careful planning, hard work and time. You can do it if you have an "I can and "I will" attitude. Commit to building a solid foundation that can sustain financial wellness and long-term success.

Stephon Lee

Chapter 5

Secure Your Position

Many people secure their homes by locking their doors and activating an alarm system. These steps are taken to reduce the risk of an intrusion and protect the home along with its most valued assets from being harmed.

Securing your finances in many ways are similar. A person should lock the doors to his or her financial assets and put in place an alarm system to sound an alert when financial danger exists.

Sound financial management is the system that help secures and keeps a person's finances from harm. Good financial management provides tight financial security and ongoing monitoring services to block dangerous activities that could lead to financial failure.

What is financial security? If you ask twenty people you would most likely get twenty different answers. Some may describe financial security as free from financial care, anxiety, danger and having a safe, dependable and firm financial situation.

Most will ultimately define financial security in terms of not having to work for an income but owning enough savings, assets or income that would sustain their desired standard of living throughout their lifetime.

For a moment, let's reflect upon Humpty's example. There were several actions that Humpty could have taken to avoid a fall. Obviously, the risk was created when Humpty climbed too high and was living above his ability to keep safe. Humpy could have reduced the risk of a fall had he secured his position.

He should have built a safe and solid foundation. Humpty needed a base that would not sway in the event of a storm or adverse condition. Unfortunately, Humpty's position was not secure. His foundation was not firm. The wind blew, the wall shook and Humpty rolled off the wall and fell.

Too many people spend excessive money on houses, cars, entertainment, clothing and so on while leaving literally nothing to help secure their financial position. When adverse and hard economic times come, they are not prepared or able to endure the challenge.

Much like Humpty, without a secure position, a fall can suddenly happen as a result of unfavorable events such as a job loss, reduction in income, illness in the family, emergency or any other unexpected financial challenges.

How should you secure your position and achieve financial security? There are two things that we will discuss in this chapter to secure your position:

1. Being debt free
2. Having adequate savings and assets (Net Worth)

One of the biggest obstacles to financial security is too much debt. There is a problem with excessive debt. Some people may not have experienced the consequences from this problem yet. However, lack of attention to excessive debt will only allow the problem to get worse. If left unresolved excessive debt could cause major financial problems in the future. In order to secure your finances aggressively reduce debts and increase savings.

The debt to income ratio is a significant financial gauge to help evaluate credit risk. A low debt to income ratio shows a person that he or she has a good balance between debt and income. High debt to income ratio is a warning sign that is alerting a person of potential financial trouble.

The example below illustrates the negative impact of debt against one's ability to secure a strong financial position.

Example #1:
John's gross income is $75,000 per year. He has $18,000 in credit card debt, $29,000 auto loan, and a $195,000 mortgage with 5% interest rate. John's monthly debt payments total $2,464. His debt to income ($2,464/$6,250) is 39.4%.

Jane gross income is $40,000 per year. She has $500 in credit card debt, no auto loan, and $65,000 mortgage with a 5% rate. Jane's monthly debt total $525. Her debt to income ratio ($525/$3,333) is 15.8%.

Based on the information provided above, even though

Jane earns a lot less than John, Jane's financial position is more secure than John's position. The primary reason is because John has a lot more debt in comparison to his income than Jane. Only 15.8% of Jane's gross income is obligated to debt payments. In the example, 39.4% of John's monthly gross income is obligated to debt payments. The higher debt to income ratio poses a higher financial risk.

Example #2:

Mike's company recently downsized its workforce. He was moved to part-time status and his income was reduced to $30,000 per year. Mike only works 20 hours per week. Mike has no debt other than a $1,200 monthly mortgage payment. Mike is 35 years old. At the end of the month Mike has $200 left over after all bills are paid. Mike currently has $55,000 in his savings account.

His coworker Linda was not affected by the company's downsizing. Linda is also 35 years old. Linda has $35,000 in debt plus a $1,500 mortgage payment. Her total debt payments are $2,500. Linda maintained a $60,000 salary. At the end of the month Linda has $400 left over after all bills are paid. Linda currently has $20,000 in her savings account.

Based on the information provided above, even though Mike earns a lot less than Linda, Mike's financial position is more secure than Linda's position. The primary reason is because Mike has lower monthly household expenses, lower debts and a lot more savings than Linda.

The first step to solve a problem is to conduct a "Financial Reality Check." In other words, do a self evaluation to truthfully determine where you are financially.

This will help you identify and plan the areas that you will need to change in order to make your finances more safe and secure. On page 45 is the "Financial Reality Check." Take a few minutes to complete the form.

The self evaluation will provide you valuable information about your debt level. The assessment is meant to help you to know 1) your debt to income ratio and 2) how you rate based on your debt level.

Financial Reality Check

Determine Your Debt to Income Ratio and Grade

It's important that you accurately provide your personal information to get a good and honest assessment.

Mortgage amount should include (principal, interest, taxes and insurance). Credit card amount should equal the required minimum monthly payment.

(A) Monthly Gross Income $ _____

Monthly Debt Payments

Home Mortgage	$ _____
Hom Equity Loan	$ _____
Auto Loan	$ _____
Credit Cards	$ _____
Student Loans	$ _____
Personal Loans	$ _____
Other Loans	$ _____

(B) Total Monthly Debt Payments $ _____

(C) Debt to Income Ratio {Divide line **(B)** by line **(A)**} _____ %

Use your "Debt to Income Ratio" from above to determine your "Debt to Income Grade". Check the box that best represents your grade.

	Debt to Income Ratio	Grade	
☐	15% or less	A	Excellent
☐	16% to 25%	B	Good
☐	26% to 40%	C	Fair
☐	Over 40%	D	Poor

Use the information from the Financial Reality Check to begin eliminating excessive debt. Knowing your debt situation is essential to being able to make the appropriate changes.

If you scored an excellent grade (Debt to Income Ratio of 15% or lower) then you are to be congratulated. Like many, you may have excess debt. If so, you can eliminate your debt over the long-term. Make it your goal and begin now taking the necessary steps to being debt-free.

Similar to the credit score, lenders look at the debt to income ratio when they are deciding whether to lend money or extend credit to someone. As previously mentioned, most lenders want you to keep your total debt to income ratio below 36%. The lower debt to income ratio indicates less potential for financial failure.

One way you can think about the debt to income ratio is that each 1% of the debt ratio represents 1¢ of a dollar. For example, if your debt to income ratio is 36% then 36¢ of every dollar you earn, would be obligated to paying your debts.

If you are in a 30% tax bracket with a 36% debt to income ratio, then 66¢ of every dollar you earn is already committed before you get your paycheck. In a scenario like this one, 34¢ of every $1 earned is left over to pay for all other expenditures including savings (.i.e. retirement, college, rainy day fund, etc.) charitable donations (.i.e. tithing, charities, etc.) additional major purchases (i.e. auto, furniture, home improvement, etc.) appliances, major repairs, routine maintenances, vacations, food, clothing, utilities, transportation costs, child care, entertainment, gift giving (i.e. birthdays, Christmas, etc.) and any other items.

The ideal debt level is 15% or less of your gross income. This may seem difficult but it can be achieved. The lower the debt load the lesser the risk of having financial trouble. Other positive factors such as a large savings can help reduce the risk of a high debt to income ratio.

For example, when someone has a very large amount of savings, in the event of a loss of income the savings could be used either to replace the income loss or pay off the debt balances.

In order to maintain a low debt to income level, you

should manage your finances so that your debt does not increase at a faster rate than your income. This is also true in the reverse. If you are expecting an income reduction because you plan to retire or take a lower salary, then your debt payments will also need to decrease.

You should decrease the debt payments at the same or faster rate than the decrease in income. If your gross income decreases faster than your debt payments, the decrease in income will result in a higher debt to income ratio than it was before the decrease in income.

An example would be Mark having a "good" debt to income ratio of 20%. Mark's gross income is $10,000 per month and his debt payments total $2,000 per month. If Mark's gross income drops to $5,000 per month and his monthly debts remain at $2,000 then, Mark's debt to income would have increased to 40%. The new debt to income ratio would be determined by the $2,000 debt payments divided by a gross monthly income of $5,000. The result of the reduction in income has caused the debt to income ratio to increase from 20% a "good score" to 40%, which is a one step away for being a "poor score." A "poor score" indicates that Mark has too much debt for his income and is in danger of having financial challenges.

In order to get rid of debt you will need a good budget. Once you develop your budget you will need to follow it. Within your budget or spending plan you will need to determine what is "a need" and what is "a want."

Going to the movies and eating out at restaurants are wants or discretionary spending. A person must have food to live but there is a more cost-effective way to meet that need. One way is to prepare meals at home, which is usually less expensive than eating out. In order to aggressively reduce debts you will need to eliminate as many "want" items as soon as possible. Then you can use those "want" or discretionary funds to eliminate debts.

Budgeting is crucial to your financial success. It will be imperative that a lot of energy is given to find ways to reduce your expenses and debts. Later in Chapter 10, "Take Action and Budget" we will address budgeting in more detail.

As you begin to aggressively eliminate debt, you should try and eliminate the debts with the higher interest cost first.

For example, if you have a credit card at 15% interest and another at 24% interest, the higher interest rate will cost you the more. The credit card with 24% interest rate will cost you more money and therefore would need to be eliminated faster than the card with the 15% interest rate.

You should reduce or eliminate the use of debt especially obtained by the use of credit cards and "buy now and pay later" programs. "Buy now and pay later" programs are frequently used to entice consumers to purchase furniture, appliances, electronics and other large dollar items. "Buy now and pay later" programs are appealing but many are traps that lock people into debts they cannot afford.

Always remember that paying the minimum gets you minimum results. Your objective is to be debt free. Your plan should be to aggressively eliminate debts. To achieve this objective, pay more than the minimum payments as often as possible.

Table I titled, "Impact above Paying Minimum" shows how paying more reduce debt faster than paying minimum payments. The calculations used in the table are based on Mike's personal debt of $3,500 with a 15.5% interest rate.

Mike is considering paying the minimum payment of $75 or increasing the payment to $150 per month to pay against his personal debt. Mike prepared Table I to compare the results of Plan 1 which is to pay $75 per month (minimum payment) verses Plan 2 which is to pay $150 per month against his personal debt.

Table I
Impact of Paying Above Minimum

	Plan 1	Plan 2
Payments	$75	$150
Month	Remaining Balance	
Beginning Balance	$3,500.00	$3,500.00
6	$3,315.38	$2,850.59
12	$3,115.98	$2,149.20
18	$2,900.61	$1,391.67
24	$2,668.01	$573.50
28	$2,502.69	$0.00

Interest Rate is 15.5% for both plans

The result of Mike's analysis shows that by paying more than the minimum payment, Mike's personal debt is completely eliminated in the 28th month with Plan 2. Plan 2 has a $0 balance and Plan 1 has a remaining balance of $2,502.69 in the 28th month.

Lesson learned from Table I
Pay more than the minimum payments against outstanding debts. The more you pay against the debt the faster the debt is paid off.

Table II titled, "Impact of Lower Interest Rates" shows how paying a lower interest rate, more of the monthly payment will can be used to pay down debt at a faster rate.

Jennifer wants to get out of debt. She prepared Table II below to help understand how a lower interest cost allows debt to be paid off faster.

The calculations used in Table II are based on Jennifer's credit card debt of $4,375. Jennifer is comparing the pay-off schedule for her credit card. Her calculation uses 23.5% interest rate in Plan 1 and 9.5% in Plan 2. Both Plan 1 and Plan 2 pay the same monthly amount of $175 against the outstanding debt.

Table II
Impact of Lower Interest Rates

	Plan 1	Plan 2
Interest Rates	23.50%	9.50%
Month	Remaining Balance	
Beginning Balance	$4,375.00	$4,375.00
6	$3,812.13	$3,515.97
12	$3,179.80	$2,615.31
18	$2,469.43	$1,671.02
24	$1,671.40	$680.98
28	$1,085.39	$0.00

Monthly payment is $175 for both plans

The result of Jennifer's analysis shows that by lowering the interest rate, Plan 2 debt balance is $0 in the 28th month. Plan 1 has a remaining debt balance of $1,085.39 in the 28th month.

The only reason Plan 2 debt balance is fully paid off in month 28th and Plan 1 has a remaining debt balance in the 28th month is because Plan 2 had a lower interest cost compared to Plan 1.

Lesson learned from Table II

Seek to lower the interest rates on your outstanding debts. By lowering the interest costs, a larger portion of each monthly payment is used to pay off the outstanding debt balance. Debts are paid off faster with lower interest rates.

If your debts are extremely delinquent, you may need to contact a credit counselor or debt management company like Consumer Credit Counseling Services (CCCS) or InCharge® Debt Solutions for assistance.

Debt management involves developing a payment plan that often includes lowered interest rates and decreased monthly payments in exchange for closing all your credit card accounts.

If a company is willing to settle a debt, accumulate the agreed upon amount and hold the funds until you are ready to settle.

Talk with your tax adviser to understand the tax consequences of taking a settlement offer. If you accept a settlement offer, make sure that you get the settlement in writing prior to sending the lump payment to satisfy the debt.

Once debts are eliminated you can begin to save more aggressively. Imagine if you own your home and car without any debt! What would be your financial outlook? How would your everyday life be different?

Some debts are advantageous. For example, debt used to buy a home that has an appreciating value could be a good use of debt. Debt creates an obligation for the borrower to repay the lender the amount borrowed plus interest at a later date. A person should carefully evaluate his or her ability to meet the potential obligation prior to acquiring debt. Even though some debt is beneficial, poor debt management can lead to a major financial problem. Given the recurring financial challenges caused by excessive debt a person should limit the use of debt.

Being debt free is a financially sound way to help secure your financial position. If you own your home and have little to no debt along with a good amount of savings, a job loss or decline in economic conditions would have lesser impact on your finances. You would have a stronger foundation to weather economic storms and adverse conditions.

As we mentioned earlier in this chapter, being able to manage your debt well is a foundational building block to secure your financial position. The second building block is having adequate savings and assets.

Inevitably, we all at some point in our lives will face an unexpected event. These emergencies can occur at the most inconvenient times. Often unexpected events cause emotional and financial stress. Establishing an emergency savings account is necessary in good times, as well as, in bad.

The better you plan the more financially prepared you will be when unforeseen events take place. When you plan for unexpected events, the financial pressure is less when the incidents occur. Planning requires putting money away "just in case" the unexpected happens.

For example, if the car water pump stops working or the roof starts leaking, the cash reserve fund will provide immediate access to money to cover the repair costs. If a family member becomes ill and out of town travel is required, having adequate cash saved would provide the money to pay the unexpected travel expense, reduce complications and minimize stress that would exist if the money was not available.

You should pay the emergency fund as if it is a bill. Your goal should be to save three to six months of your income in an emergency fund to be prepared for unexpected events.

Put the money away and don't be tempted by the latest sale. Stashing money in a checking account takes a lot of discipline. Money in a checking account is hard to accumulate because it is readily accessible and easy to spend using your debit card or checkbook. There are loads of demands and temptations coming at you – the mortgage, car payment, taxes, sales at the mall, eating out, and so many other fun and interesting things.

Savings strategies, such as automatic monthly payroll deductions are successful because the money comes out of your paycheck before you can get your hands on it. Whether a person is putting money away for emergencies or retirement having funds automatically deducted from his or her paycheck is a good way to save.

Saving money should be a part of your budget. Each dollar saved by reducing expenses should be used first to eliminate high cost debts and second to fund cash reserves and long-term saving plans.

The sooner a person starts saving for retirement the better. The following example helps to show the value of compounding interest. The earlier a person starting saving the sooner compounding interest begins to work in his or her favor.

For example, Linda is 25 years old. She saves $500 per month in a retirement account until age of 60 with a 5% compound interest rate being applied to the balance. In 35 years, Linda's account balance would have accrued to $568,046.21. On the other hand, Mike waited and started his retirement saving at 35 years old. He will also save $500 per month in a retirement account until he reaches the age of 60 with a 5% compound interest rate being applied to the balance. In 25 years, Mike's account balance would have accrued to $297,754.85.

In comparison, Mike delayed starting his retirement

saving by 10 years compared to Linda. They each saved $500 per month and earned 5% on the investments. Linda would contribute $60,000 more to her retirement plan than Mike. The additional 10 years of savings would increase Linda's retirement account by $270,291.36 more than Mike's retirement account balance. Linda's retirement account would be almost twice the amount of Mike's retirement account. By not delaying 10 years, Linda acquired a net gain of $210,291.36 greater than what Mike accumulated at the age of 60 years old.

Linda's net gain over Mike is a result of "money earning money" from the effect of compounding interest.

It is the same principle (compounding interest) in reverse used for the calculation of your home mortgage. For example, if you borrowed $175,000 at a 5% fixed rate for 30 years, the total amount of interest and principle would be paid is $338,197.65 over the life of a 30 years mortgage. The total amount you would pay (including principle and interest) is almost twice the amount you borrowed for the home.

Compounding interest when applied against the outstanding balance will increase the balance of the investment or debt. Ideally, you want to be the investor (the one who saves money) instead of the borrower. As the investor the power of compounding interest works for you and not against you.

Unfortunately, too many people are not adequately planning or saving. It is easy to procrastinate in starting a saving plan. There are real costs and risk in delaying your saving plan.

Most companies offer retirement saving programs such as a 401k plan. The 403(b) plan is a retirement plan for employees of tax-exempt organizations like public schools, hospitals and nonprofit organizations. Many employers match a portion of the funds the employee contributes to the plan. You should take advantage of your employer's matching program. This is an excellent way to help build your retirement savings. There are also Individual Retirement Accounts (IRA) saving plans that can be considered for retirement savings. Individuals should talk with their tax advisers to determine eligibility and the best options given the tax consideration.

Don't be like Humpty Dumpty. He did not secure his position. Maybe, Humpty was planning to secure his position but he waited too late. He left himself exposed to unnecessary risks. Remember what happened to Humpty. The wind blew, the wall shook, and Humpty rolled off the wall and fell to his demise. This unexpected tragedy may have been avoided with proper planning. Having a solid and firm foundation is essential to protecting yourself against the unforeseeable.

This does not have to happen to you. Start preparing now so that when the storms come, you are financially secure and well positioned by having little to no debt, adequate emergency funds, and long-term savings to endure the worst of times.

The next several chapters will provide additional financial insight to help you to eliminate debt and better your financial position.

Stephon Lee

Chapter 6

Create a Safety Net

Sound financial planning must include a safety net. If Humpty Dumpty had planned a safety net to help protect him in the event of a fall, possibly it could have made the difference. Having proper insurance provides a safety net to help protect valuable assets in the event of an unexpected or unpleasant situation.

Who really knows why Humpty could not be put back together again? Perhaps Humpty did not have medical insurance to pay his medical bills. As a result, the king's men could not put him back together again.

Secondly, when Humpty fell, did he have a disability plan? If not, a hard fall could have financially disabled Humpty. Imagine what it would have been like for

Humpty after the fall having to experience the physical pain, loss of income and no health insurance. The financial burden alone would have amassed until it overwhelmed him.

When we fail to plan or do the things we should, often we unintentionally burden those who love us the most. We leave them with resolving an unexpected difficult situation. The greatest responsibility rests with the one needing the insurance.

In advance of a major problem, look within your budget and find ways to cut expenses to buy the insurance you need. A lack of adequate insurance coverage could leave you and your family with a major financial problem.

Whenever possible, seek to secure a health insurance plan. If money is tight and you cannot afford full coverage then consider a high-deductible health plan (HDHP). Given the financial and physical devastation that could potentially occur from a major illness, having health insurance is critical. It provides a safety net.

Having health insurance is crucial to protecting individuals from falling too deep into unpaid medical bills.

Without health coverage, for many, their lives would be the Humpty Dumpty story where the pieces could not be put back together again.

If you do not have health insurance and you are going to need your family financial support, it is better to have the family to help pay the monthly health insurance premiums rather than the huge and surmounting cost of unpaid major medical bills that would result from not having health insurance.

Humpty Dumpty's fall had additional ramifications for those that depended upon him. If Humpty did not have life insurance, his loved ones would not only have the sorrow of losing Humpty but also the financial burden that Humpty would have left behind.

Assuming Humpty did not have life insurance to meet his spouse's and little Humpty Dumpties' current and future needs, Humpty's fall would have ended in a bigger misfortune than we know. The sadness and disappointment of this story goes beyond Humpty's fall and the regret of those who did not save him.

Who knows what happened to his family given their

dependence upon Humpty's income to pay the mortgage and other household bills? Humpty's fall could have left his family without an income resulting in the ultimate consequence of the family losing their home to foreclosure.

If the family was left without an income then who would pay for the dreams of his children growing up in their neighborhood and attending a college of their choice? Surrounded by an unstable environment, the financial stress of all the events including the financial worries may have overwhelmed the family and caused much more grief than we understand.

Unfortunately, the ill-fated circumstances that would follow Humpty's fall were the result of Humpty's not having the safety net for his family. Humpty could have protected his income simply with a life insurance policy.

We should not practice Humpty Dumpty finances with our lives, family or with others who depend upon us. We should do all we can to make sure that our financial plan includes adequate insurance. Adequate insurance includes life, medical, auto, home, renters and disability.

Having proper insurance is very important. If your

employer offers group insurance benefits at a cost savings, you should take advantage of the employee benefit plan. If you are planning to change jobs, you may consider buying an individual life policy that you own.

It is wise to meet with an insurance professional to discuss your overall insurance needs. A good insurance agent will be able to help you determine your insurance needs.

A life insurance agent can help you secure the amount of life insurance to fully cover the needs of the surviving spouse and children in the event of a premature death. If your budget is tight, you may want to consider purchasing a term life insurance policy.

It is wise not to delay the purchase of life insurance when it is needed to protect your love ones. A term policy is life coverage only. There is no saving component with term life insurance. The money you pay for the policy goes only to the cost of the insurance. On the death of the insured it pays the face amount of the policy to the person named as the beneficiary. Term life policy is one of the low cost plans for life coverage. Your life insurance agent should be able to discuss the best options for you.

A property and casualty agent can help you obtain insurance to protect your properties such as your home, automobile, furniture, and etc. Most homeowner's insurance premium payments are included with the mortgage payments.

If you rent an apartment, it is very important to take out insurance on your personal property. Insurance is important not only for a homeowner but also for renters. In the case of a fire, burglary, internal flooding, pipes bursting, sewage backup or some other type of unforeseen event that results in your personal property being lost, you would then have Renter's Insurance coverage that will help you quickly recover the loss.

Having adequate insurance is sound financial planning. But what should you do if you do not have enough money to pay for the insurance? As mentioned earlier in this chapter, review your budget. Look for ways to increase income or reduces expenses. You should make budget adjustments to find the money needed to purchase insurance.

If your budget is tight, you will need to talk with your

insurance professional to objectively discuss your risks and options. We will discuss budgeting in more details in Chapter 10, "Take Action and Budget."

Along with your insurance planning make sure you prepare a will. Regardless of how little or how much money you have, preparing a will allows you to direct your personal belongings and assets to the family members or loved ones you have designated.

In the event there is not a written will, State Inheritance Laws will dictate who will inherit the assets from an estate. The need for a will is even greater if you have young children that depend upon your care. Having a will prepared is a necessity so that a guardian is identified for your children. The will helps to ensure that your loved ones are cared for according to your plans in the event of an unexpected death.

The cost to prepare a simple will can be as little as $200 or less. Costs vary based on the complexity of the will. The more complex your assets or circumstances, the more an attorney will charge for the service. For an estate with significant assets, the cost could be as much as $5,000 or more. You can go online to search for legal services and compare prices. You should verify the trustworthiness of the legal services prior to securing it. Use a source such as the Better Business Bureau to verify the service's standing. It is free and provides an updated list of the services standing and any registered complaints and resolutions.

The key to success is to know the right things to do and take the appropriate actions. Many times we delay doing what is in the best interest of loved ones, family, friends and ourselves. Change occurs when we take responsibility for the outcome. Sometimes change is not easy.

If you do not have an adequate safety net for you and your family, set a specific date now to get it done. Schedule a date and time as to when you will secure sufficient insurance protection for you and your family. You and your family will be glad that you took the time to do so.

HumptyDumptyFinances.com has some additional tools, resources and ways to help you find insurances or save money on your insurances. Take a moment and visit the website.

Chapter 7

Simplify Your Finances

Eliminate Debt

Begin to eliminate as much outstanding debt as possible.

Pay off as much outstanding debt as you can on your credit cards, vehicles, personal loans, home mortgage and any other debts. Determine to apply any extra money you receive to pay off debt. This will simplify your finances and reduce your interest payments.

Credit cards act somewhat like doors that give commercial enterprises on the outside access to your financial resources. In order for you to control access, close all unnecessary doors and lock them. Extra credit cards are a temptation to spend more money.

As a general rule, keep only one or two credit cards at most. Pay off and close credit card accounts that are not absolutely necessary. Send written notice to the credit card company stating your desire to close the account. You should keep a copy in your personal files. Make sure to request a final statement that shows a "0" (zero) balance.

If you currently have more than two credit cards, make a plan to close out all extra cards. There are two methods for paying off credit card balances.

1. Pay off the credit cards with the lowest balances first.

2. Pay off the credit cards with highest interest rates first.

Paying off the credit cards with the highest interest rate first, provides the highest cost savings. However, many people prefer paying off the credit cards with lowest balance first in order to achieve the immediate gratification of having a credit card balance fully paid off.

Once you have paid off the credit card balance, communicate in writing to the credit card company stating your desire to close that account. Follow this procedure with your other cards until you have closed the accounts on all cards except one or two at the most.

If one or more of your current credit cards has a significantly higher rate of interest than the others, it would be better to focus on eliminating the outstanding balance for that account first even though it may be more gratifying to have the smaller balance paid off first.

For example, if you had a credit card with a lower balance of $1,000 with a 12% interest rate verses a credit card with a balance of $3,000 with 19.5% interest, it would be better to pay off the $3,000 balance first. The credit card with the 19.5% interest rate is much higher than the 12% rate on the credit card with the lower balance.

It is always best to pay off the credit cards with the higher interest rate first when it is significantly higher. The large difference in rates makes the savings greater when you pay off the higher rates credit cards first.

You may also be able to roll the outstanding balance in the account that carries a higher interest rate over to another account with a lower rate of interest by writing a check from the account with the lower rate of interest to close out the balance of the one with the higher interest rate. You should check for hidden fees that may be associated with a transfer of balance from one card to another. If there are substantial fees, the cost savings may not be enough to justify transferring the balance from the higher interest to the lower interest credit card.

Only use credit cards for particular department stores if you make regular purchases of necessary items at those places and the credit card provides you a clear financial benefit such as price discounts or lower interest charges. Keeping credit cards for stores that sell luxury items are a temptation to spend money on unnecessary items. Stores continuously send advertisements to those who have their credit cards. These solicitations can distract you and take your focus off your personal financial plan.

Write your creditor stating your intent to close your credit card account. Include in the letter your request for a final statement reflecting the zero balance. At a future point, obtain an updated credit report to verify that your credit file shows the closed account, zero balance and that the account reflects closed by borrower.

Discard any offers for new credit cards that may come to you in the mail unless they provide a significant and long-term financial benefit, such as lower interest rates or credits on the purchase of necessary goods or services. But, if you open a new account, you should eliminate an existing account.

It is good to request a credit report from the three credit reporting agencies at least one time per year to find out what information is in your credit file. It is important that the information in your file be correct because potential employers and credit institutions may review that information when applying for employment or credit. You may find some surprises in your file. If there are errors in your file, instruct the company to correct them. HumptyDumptyFinances.com has more information and helpful resources pertaining to your credit.

After you have reviewed and corrected your credit files, you can write the credit reporting agencies and request them to place a "file block for solicitation purposes" in your credit file. This will prohibit the credit reporting agencies from selling your name and considerably reduce the amount of mail solicitation that you receive.

By eliminating debt we simplify our lives. We remove the financial burden, risks, and ongoing administrative tasks associated with debt. As we eliminate debt we are able to more aggressively save and build a brighter and more solid financial future. Without excessive debt we are more financially secure and have greater financial freedom. Imagine the exhilarating feeling on the day when there are no more mortgages, auto or student loans, credit cards or any other debts to be paid because you are debt free. While some can only imagine others are living debt free each and every day.

What freedom would you experience knowing that your income is no longer obligated to debt payments? Instead of paying debts you would be free to use your money any way you choose. Many would find this financial freedom a release from anxiety, a path to new careers and business opportunities, a way to visit places only dreamed about or the ability to help others. With all the intangible and tangible benefits of being debt-free then why are so many people choosing to stay in debt?

The answer is simple. Being debt free requires a person to make a decision, commit to a plan of action and remain disciplined enough to sacrifices their wants, live within their means, deny the impulse to spend, delay unnecessary purchases, and stay on course until the debts are paid in full.

Instead many borrow until they cannot borrow anymore. Their control mechanism is when the creditor denies their next request for additional debt. This is a tragic and unfortunate way of managing your finances. There is no better time to start than now. Make the decision and commit to becoming debt free.

Stephon Lee

Chapter 8

Relieve the Pain

Just because you experience emotional pain and stress from your financial situation does not mean you are insane. Financial stress and emotional pain are normal in the midst of major financial challenges.

During your financial journey, the difficulties may cause you to laugh and at times even cry. We were created with emotions to help express the way we feel. Still, through the tears and the laughter, it is important to stay focused and continue to rebuild and create a standard of living that is well within your income.

Often people relieve the emotional pain at the shopping mall. They go shopping to buy themselves something nice to ease the pain caused by their financial problems. This is comparable to an alcoholic taking a drink to relieve the stress of abstinence. You should not go shopping to relieve the pain. You may end up buying things you do not need or cannot afford. It would only make the financial problem worse.

Putting your finances back together may be difficult, but this problem was not created overnight and fixing it may not be quick. Reducing your debts will require great sacrifice. Also, having too much debt will require great sacrifice.

The sacrifice of having too much debt verses the cost of avoiding debt is much greater. You will have to choose between living in debt and taking actions to reduce the debt. The cost of excessive debt is potential stress, a lack of peace, and financial ruin that affects not only you but your family as well.

Setting realistic goals and budgeting will help you stay motivated, focused and clear about your objectives. Attack the problem daily by sticking with your budget and following a sound plan. One of the mistakes that you do not want to make is to overwhelm yourself with the problem by looking too far ahead.

Once you identify the problem and the appropriate solution, work the plan on a daily basis. Keep your expenses under control each day. Use the "Daily Expense Tracker Form" provided in Chapter 12, "Tools to Get Started" to assist with tracking and controlling your daily expenses. This will help you to see progress immediately.

As you see progress day by day, you will gain a better understanding that your journey to recovery will take many steps. The steps you take each day are similar and will need to be repeated daily until you step out of debt. Seeing daily progress will also help build the confidence you need to endure the journey to financial recovery and wellness.

You may find additional comfort by participating in groups (such as local church groups) that can provide additional support to help you stay focused on your goals as you work towards rebuilding and restoring your finances and lifestyle.

It is important to maintain a balance in your life that includes church, family, friends and extracurricular activities. This will help preserve normalcy, reduce stress, and refresh you with the energy to handle the daily financial challenges and achieve your desired financial outcome.

Confession may be good for the soul. But, if you are going to share your financial concerns with others, it is very important that you select those who are trustworthy, caring and can maintain your personal information in confidentiality. Talking with a close friend or family member at times may be comforting. Remember that once the conversation ends the work must continue.

Friends and family may be a good source of encouragement; however, nothing will get done unless you use your energy to focus and continue working towards achieving your financial goals. The decision and responsibility for the final outcome depends primarily upon you.

The road to financial recovery and living debt free could be a lengthy and emotional journey. For some, the emotional stress is harder to deal with than others.

Having a support team that understands and is willing to talk with you during the most difficult times is valuable.

If you do not have family and friends who you can share with during your most difficult times, seek a church or nonprofit organization in your local community for help.

Resolving your problem will require focus and sound planning. As we discussed in Chapter 1, "Make the Decision" it is very important that you acknowledge the challenge, make a decision of confidence and take definitive action to resolve the problem. These actions are motivational and rewarding.

In many cases, as you take positive steps merely the fact of knowing that you have actually done what you were thinking about doing is inspirational. This reality of knowing that finally you have begun working to resolve your financial problems often provide the renewed excitement and energy necessary to continue moving forward.

If you have not completed the Personal Journal in Chapter 1, you should consider taking a moment to do so at this point.

Stephon Lee

Chapter 9

Having Adequate Income

Another building block to secure your financial position is having adequate income.

Having the ability to maintain adequate income is necessary for financial security. How do you maintain continuous and sufficient income? For most individuals, their income is maintained through continuous employment. There are things that should be done to promote stable employment. Obviously, an employee should do the work required to meet or exceed the job performance.

Here are few more things a person should consider doing to help protect and promote his or her income.

1. Maintain competitive job skills

2. Pursue additional training, certifications or advance degrees
3. Improve resume and marketing skills
4. Build quality relationships with employees from other companies
5. Eliminate employment barriers caused by poor credit score and excessive debt

It is very important that you maintain competitive job skills, unless your debts are eliminated and you have accumulated enough savings to financially support you and your family without having to work.

You should take advantage of opportunities to increase your job skills and knowledge. This should include pursuing an advanced degree or obtaining special certifications to support your resume. The more you develop your skills the less you are at risk of being harmed by a sudden job loss or need to change jobs. It's always better to be ahead and significantly prepared for the unexpected.

Knowing how to market yourself to an employer is essential to protecting and growing your income. It is crucial that you know how to write and target your resume to the specific job you may be seeking. You may consider hiring a good resume writer to guide you through this process.

The cost of a well written resume could be well worth the money. As mentioned in Chapter 2, make sure your team is very competent. Check around for referrals and get references to verify that you have a well qualified resume writer to help you with your resume.

Learn how to network with others to increase the opportunity to change job or careers when necessary. More employers are seeking new employees from referrals.

By building good relationship with other employees of companies that you may have future interest in pursuing could prove very beneficial in the long run. Employees that have a good working relationship with their employer could provide a good reference for you to their company.

The caveat is that unless a person demonstrates and maintains a good reputation, someone may not be willing or comfortable in making the referral and connection to their employer. Generally speaking, if a person has financial problems, most employees would not want to make the referral or be associated with a potentially negative issue.

The reality is that financial problems can become a major stumbling block in various ways including an encumbrance to employment. Financial issues can negatively affect a person's ability to maintain or grow their income.

Do all you can to increase and maintain an excellent credit score not only for better interest rates and lower cost of debt but also to eliminate any barriers that could prevent a potential employer from hiring you.

If you have experienced financial problems, use the principles in this book to help rebuild a solid financial future. As mentioned in Chapter 1, make the commitment and start on the road to financial recovery. Even if the journey is long and hard, giving up is not the right choice. Striving to make a positive change is the right thing to do.

For those who have excellent credit use the principles of

this book to avoid the debt trap. Make the appropriate sacrifices to stay out of debt. It may seem inconvenient but the payoff is extraordinary. If it sounds too good to be true, talk with someone who is burdened with debt and listen to their hardship story. There are many who wish they could have managed their finances a lot differently. Secure your finances by adhering to sound financial habits and enjoy the rewards of living debt free.

What if you are a business owner and do not have adequate income to secure your financial position?

The dynamics of a business owner are different than that of an employee. The issues that could prohibit a business owner from having adequate income are numerous and could range from an unrealistic business model to low performance of management or poor products and services. If you are a business owner, consider seeking a reputable financial adviser to talk with you about your business. A competent adviser can help you to objectively evaluate your business, develop a business plan and advise you on the various issues significant to running a successful business. In the meantime, you may have to consider taking a part time or full time job to assist you with your living expenses.

Stephon Lee

Chapter 10

Take Action and Budget

Every day people make financial decisions without planning or thought. Many of these choices result in buying expensive items without considering the overall plan, purpose or need for them. Much money is wasted each day due to impulsive buying.

When spending money, thought should be given to whether the purchase is needed. When we fail to carefully and wisely evaluate our spending decisions, we subject ourselves to excessive debt, bad credit and no savings, which ultimately could lead to financial ruin.

The best decisions are made with careful consideration. Making spontaneous decisions can be dangerous. Did Humpty make a quick decision the day he chose to sit upon the wall? Did Humpty consider the risk? Did Humpty give his decision much thought or was it a spur-of-the-moment decision? Why was Humpty Dumpty sitting on the wall? What was his plan or purpose?

How often do we buy things we don't need or never thought about whether we needed the item or not? We often buy too much of something or pay too much for things that would cost less with proper planning.

A budget is simply a plan for spending money. By creating a budget, a person can better control impulse spending. Part of the planning process will require making decisions on what is a "need" and what is a "want."

A simple example of planning is shopping with a list. Whether you are buying groceries or buying a house, you should write down the items to be purchased along with set limits on the spending. The more you learn to plan your purchases the better you will stay within your budget.

Budgeting is a process that starts by setting spending targets to stay within a person's means to pay bills. A personal budget is useful in controlling personal expenses. Budgeting also helps to identify spending leaks so a person can know where his or her money is going. Unless the leaks are identified and sealed, a person may discover that at the end of the month he or she is out of money, goals are not met and some bills are not paid.

There is a cost for not properly planning and budgeting. That cost is high debt, low savings and a lot of stress. Think about it. Who needs an overload of debt and stress in their lives? It is better to shop reasonably, not over spend, stay within budget, have money left over to pay bills on time and avoid the headaches of dealing everyday with creditors because you do not have the money to pay your debts.

It is very important to set goals. Goals help set direction and focus in a person's finances. By having goals such as reducing debt, saving for a vacation, college and or retirement a person is more likely to budget on an ongoing basis. A person's desire to reach his or her goals will be additional motivation for budgeting. Successful budgeting will help a person reach his or her goals.

For example, you want to eliminate a $1,200 debt within

twelve months. Based on that specific goal, your budget would need to include an additional $100 per month to be used to eliminate the debt. Once the budget is set, your actual spending should stay in line with the budget in order to achieve your financial goal. Having a goal and a spending plan will help increase a person's chance of controlling spending, paying bills on time, reducing debts and increasing savings.

If you created a budget and the expenditures are more than the monthly income you will need to begin making adjustments.

The first place to start is with the expenses that can be reduced the easiest and the fastest. These are usually the variable or discretionary costs such as entertainment and food costs. Perhaps, you will no longer be able to afford the cable bill or eating out at restaurants.

You many need to bring your lunch to work. You may need to reduce the daily miscellaneous cost of spending $2 or $3 on coffee and snacks. These miscellaneous costs can easily add up to over $100 a month. Instead of taking the family to a movie, you may have to stay in and rent a movie. There are many ways to reduce your costs.

You will need to go over your budget line by line and determine where you can cut costs.

Other areas where you can find savings for example are using coupons, buying more generic brands, and switching to a more vegetarian diet, which is usually less expensive and healthier than meats and other breaded foods. You may change your behavior and reduce utility costs by cooking less, using fewer lights, lowering the thermostat in the winter and raising the thermostat during the summer. Review your phone bills for savings and bundling advantages.

You may find that you will need to modify your shopping habits and buy less name brand. Instead buy clothing that is functional, yet still maintains the fashion and style appropriate for work. You may consider buying some of your clothing from thrift stores. Shopping at thrift stores can save a tremendous amount of money on clothing. Many times you can find clothing that have not been or barely worn. Set a limit on birthday and special holiday buying. Give the gift of love and creativity on Christmas instead of spending money you cannot afford. Maintain your credit and look for ways to reduce your interest costs on your debts, if possible. Use your savings to reduce higher costing debts, which would lower interest costs and ultimately improve your budget.

Once you have reviewed all your variable cost items, you may discover that your expenses still exceed your income. At this point you will need to tackle the more difficult items. These items are usually fixed costs that are harder to reduce.

For example, you may discover that you will need to lower your housing cost or eliminate an automobile. Reducing your housing cost whether you are paying rent or mortgage is more difficult. If you own a home, it may mean refinancing your mortgage to reduce the monthly payments or even selling your home and buying one that is more affordable. There are other options that can be considered, such as renting part of your home to a friend who is able to share the housing cost. Obviously, choosing to bring a roommate into your home will require careful consideration so that you do not create other liabilities and costs that outweigh the benefits.

It is imperative that prior to making a long-term purchase you consider all potential costs that will be incurred as a result of the new purchase.

For example, when buying a new home, your budget should not only include the mortgage payments (principal, interest, taxes, and insurances) but also other fees that could be associated with the home such as:

- ✓ management associations dues
- ✓ increase in utilities
- ✓ utility deposits required for connections
- ✓ functional interior items such as curtains and curtain rods
- ✓ appliances and equipment such as lawn equipment, refrigerators, washers, and dryers
- ✓ planned furniture purchases
- ✓ increases in incidental costs, such as food and cooking utensils associated with the accommodation and entertaining of guests

When buying a new car you should consider more than the monthly car payment. Also consider the cost of auto insurance, car title and registration, maintenance, and cost of gas. These costs could tremendously increase the cost of the car to the point that the car is not affordable.

Making the right decision will help secure your financial position. Failing to budget can lead to a major financial problem. Many people get into serious financial trouble because they do not create a budget before making a major purchase or long-term commitment such as buying a house or car.

Financial success can be achieved. Even though the path to financial success is as simple as setting goals and following a sound financial plan, many people fail to do it because it requires discipline.

One of the major obstacles to successful financial management is a lack of discipline. Discipline is a person's ability to control his or her actions. In order to successfully budget and make major progress financially a person will need to be able to stick with a plan and make the necessary sacrifices.

The problem is that too many people lack discipline and will not follow a plan. They buy what they want and whenever they want to. In most cases in order for people to reduce debt and save money they will have to buy more of what they "need" and less of what they "want."

Prudent behavior and self-control is required in order to build a solid financial future.

Often when credit becomes available, careful considerations disappear, emotional impulses take control and spending gets out of control. The spending does not stop until the lenders refuse to extend anymore credit. By the time, the person is in financial trouble.

Another important factor to financial success is income. Inherent in the budgeting process is the matching of income and expenses. Budgeting helps a person manage within their means, especially their income. Unless a person has sufficient savings and do not need to work, his or her income will be necessary to rebuild and establish a solid foundation for long-term financial success. Securing sufficient income may be a difficult step. However, we cannot be surprised or discouraged about this potential challenge. Securing adequate income may be the biggest hurdle some will face in putting their finances back together again.

Having a made-up mind is essential to not quitting but pushing to accomplish each step necessary to rebuilding. There are several things you may need to consider in order to secure adequate income.

This topic was discussed in Chapter 9, "Having Adequate Income." Some of the points are restated in this chapter. If you do not have a job, you need to first ensure that you have a good resume and interview skills. Talk with others who are skilled in this area to help make improvements needed to enhance your chance of getting the job.

Secondly, if additional income is needed, a second job may be necessary. Talking to others to inquire about job openings and networking opportunities are always helpful. If necessary, you may need to be retrained or consider another area of work in order to enhance your job opportunities.

If you do not have adequate income, you should make seeking income a full time effort. Adequate income is needed to support and ensure a full recovery and ongoing financial wellness. Work an extra job to help pay your debts and improve your finances. This option may be worth the consideration. Take courses to improve your educational background. It is very important that you continue to improve your skills and training to make yourself more valuable to a potential employer.

In order to successfully budget, exercise diligence to avoid excessive debts and over indulging in buying things that are not necessary. Maintain a balance in every financial decision. Educate and share with all in your household, including spouse and children the need to be financial sound. If you lack understanding in financial matters, seek wise counsel. But do not sign and engage in a financial transaction that you do not understand. Keep your finances simple. Live as much as possible being debt free and on a budget.

HumptyDumptyFinances.com has some additional tools, resources and ways to help you budget. Take a moment and visit the website.

Stephon Lee

Chapter 11

Seven Points to Remember

In summary, there are many things Humpty Dumpty could have done to protect himself from a fall. There are seven key points to remember.

1. Financial success can be achieved. It will require you to make the decision, stay committed and take the necessary actions to reach your goals.

2. Seek sound advice from qualified and competent advisers. Having wise counsel and good financial information will empower you to make better financial decisions.

3. It is very important that as soon as you see that you are having trouble paying your bills that you

ask for help. Don't wait. It is easier to help prevent a fall than to make major repairs after the fall has occurred.

4. Living above your means will most certainly position you for a fall. When you are spending in excess of your income, you are living above your means, which will eventually lead to a fall.

5. One of the biggest obstacles to financial security is too much debt. If left unresolved, excessive debt will lead to financial trouble. Aggressively reducing debts and increasing savings will help secure your finances.

6. Sound financial planning must include a safety net. Having insurance (health, life, home, auto and disability) provides a safety net to help protect valuable assets in the event of an unexpected or unpleasant situation.

7. By eliminating debt you simplify your life. You remove the financial burden, risks, and ongoing administrative tasks associated with debt.

Chapter 12

Tools to Get Started

In this section, we will provide tools that you can use to better manage your finances.

Before starting with the tools, we will share a few common sense tips. The following tips should be put into practice in order to avoid financial challenges.

- ✓ Pay your taxes – avoid getting in tax trouble. Know that the Internal Revenue Service (IRS) is not your enemy. Comply with the IRS due date and filing requirements. If you are having difficulty with paying your taxes, contact the IRS to arrange a payment plan.

- ✓ File your taxes on time – avoid creating

unnecessary penalties. If you need additional time to file your tax return, apply for an extension. This is even more crucial for a business return.

✓ Small business owners – make sure that all payroll taxes are filed and paid on time. Refuse to borrow money from the payroll taxes withheld from the employees. Many small businesses create huge tax penalties and get in trouble with the IRS because payroll taxes withheld from employees are not paid timely.

✓ Get routine physical examinations – avoid health problems by having a regular check up to ensure that you are in good health. Routine medical exams can help you stay on top of your health condition. You should make appropriate corrections as recommended by your professional medical adviser. High medical costs caused by poor medical attention can lead to financial challenges.

✓ Regularly exercise - physical fitness is also very important to good health and it can help prevent unnecessary medical costs and out of pocket expenditures. Your finances are better preserved when a person maintains good health. Proper physical fitness can help lower your out of pocket costs.

✓ Maintain proper diet – like physical fitness, proper dieting is necessary and should be done. Eating the wrong foods are higher costs to your budget as well as to your health. Eat a well balanced diet. There are many websites you can visit to learn about good eating habits.

Below are tools to help you budget. You can use the worksheets provided within this book daily to track your expenses. These tools are simple and easy to use.

1. Begin on Day 1 using the diary on page 110.

2. Use the diary to begin writing down your thoughts and plans as to how you can and will improve your finances.

3. Use the Expense Tracker to log your daily purchases to get an idea of where your money is

going.

4. Log your daily expenditures for 30 days consecutively. This should be adequate time to provide an idea of your spending habits. By tracking your daily expenditures, you will be able to see how you are spending your money and get better control over your expenditures.

You can go online to <u>www.humptydumptyfinances.com</u> to find additional resources to help you budget. Online budgeting tools and software are available on Humpty Dumpty Finances' website.

Starting Day 1

Week 1

Diary for the Week

Today's Date: _____

Goal for the Week:

_____

_____

Payments due for the Week:

_____

_____

_____

Saving Ideas for the Week:

_____

_____

_____

Log – Thoughts, Reminders, and Accomplishments:

_____

_____

_____

_____

_____

_____

_____

Weekly Expense Tracker Form

Line Item	Date	Description of Money Spent For example: Purchased groceries, lunch at fast food restaurant, snacks, gasoline, oil change and gifts. Paid electric bill and etc.	Amount
1			$
2			$
3			$
4			$
5			$
6			$
7			$
8			$
9			$
10			$
11			$
12			$
13			$
14			$
15			$
16			$
17			$
18			$
19			$
20			$
Sub-Total 1			$

Go to next page and continue to log expenses for the week.

Weekly Expense Tracker Form

Line Item	Date	Description of Money Spent For example: Purchased groceries, lunch at fast food restaurant, snacks, gasoline, oil change and gifts. Paid electric bill and etc.	Amount
21			$
22			$
23			$
24			$
25			$
26			$
27			$
28			$
29			$
30			$
31			$
32			$
33			$
34			$
35			$
36			$
37			$
38			$
39			$
40			$
Sub-Total 2			$

Summary for the Week

Weekly Expense Tracker

    Sub-total 1 $_____

    Sub-total 2 $_____

    Total Expenses for the Week $_____

Check each box that summarizes your week's activities

- ☐ Used the Expense Tracker for the week
- ☐ Found ways to cut costs
- ☐ Paid bills on time
- ☐ Used coupons and discounts to save money
- ☐ Reduced use of credit cards
- ☐ Stayed on track with efforts to become debt-free
- ☐ Helped friends and family to start the Humpty's fitness plan

Notes – Weekly Activities and Achievements

_____
_____
_____
_____
_____

Books for Humpty financial fitness program can be ordered at
www.HumptyDumptyFinances.com

Expense Scratch Pad

(Week that Begins _____)

Expense Item _____			Expense Item _____			Expense Item _____		
Line	Amount		Line	Amount		Line	Amount	
_____	$ _____		_____	$ _____		_____	$ _____	
_____	$ _____		_____	$ _____		_____	$ _____	
_____	$ _____		_____	$ _____		_____	$ _____	
_____	$ _____		_____	$ _____		_____	$ _____	
_____	$ _____		_____	$ _____		_____	$ _____	
	$ _____			$ _____			$ _____	

Expense Item _____			Expense Item _____			Expense Item _____		
Line	Amount		Line	Amount		Line	Amount	
_____	$ _____		_____	$ _____		_____	$ _____	
_____	$ _____		_____	$ _____		_____	$ _____	
_____	$ _____		_____	$ _____		_____	$ _____	
_____	$ _____		_____	$ _____		_____	$ _____	
_____	$ _____		_____	$ _____		_____	$ _____	
	$ _____			$ _____			$ _____	

Expense Item _____			Expense Item _____			Expense Item _____		
Line	Amount		Line	Amount		Line	Amount	
_____	$ _____		_____	$ _____		_____	$ _____	
_____	$ _____		_____	$ _____		_____	$ _____	
_____	$ _____		_____	$ _____		_____	$ _____	
_____	$ _____		_____	$ _____		_____	$ _____	
_____	$ _____		_____	$ _____		_____	$ _____	
	$ _____			$ _____			$ _____	

Starting Day 8

Week 2

Diary for the Week

Today's Date: _____

Goal for the Week:

_____

_____

Payments due for the Week:

_____

_____

_____

Saving Ideas for the Week:

_____

_____

_____

Log – Thoughts, Reminders, and Accomplishments:

_____

_____

_____

_____

_____

_____

Weekly Expense Tracker Form

		Description of Money Spent	
Line Item	Date	For example: Purchased groceries, lunch at fast food restaurant, snacks, gasoline, oil change and gifts. Paid electric bill and etc.	Amount
1			$
2			$
3			$
4			$
5			$
6			$
7			$
8			$
9			$
10			$
11			$
12			$
13			$
14			$
15			$
16			$
17			$
18			$
19			$
20			$
Sub-Total 1			$

Go to next page and continue to log expenses for the week.

Weekly Expense Tracker Form

Line Item	Date	Description of Money Spent For example: Purchased groceries, lunch at fast food restaurant, snacks, gasoline, oil change and gifts. Paid electric bill and etc.	Amount
21			$
22			$
23			$
24			$
25			$
26			$
27			$
28			$
29			$
30			$
31			$
32			$
33			$
34			$
35			$
36			$
37			$
38			$
39			$
40			$
Sub- Total 2			**$**

Summary for the Week

Weekly Expense Tracker

    Sub-total 1 $_____

    Sub-total 2 $_____

    Total Expenses for the Week $_____

Check each box that summarizes your week's activities

- ☐ Used the Expense Tracker for the week
- ☐ Found ways to cut costs
- ☐ Paid bills on time
- ☐ Used coupons and discounts to save money
- ☐ Reduced use of credit cards
- ☐ Stayed on track with efforts to become debt-free
- ☐ Helped friends and family to start the Humpty's fitness plan

Notes – Weekly Activities and Achievements

_____

_____

_____

_____

_____

Books for Humpty financial fitness program can be ordered at
www.HumptyDumptyFinances.com

Expense Scratch Pad

(Week that Begins _____)

Expense Item _____			Expense Item _____			Expense Item _____		
Line	Amount		Line	Amount		Line	Amount	
____	$_____		____	$_____		____	$_____	
____	$_____		____	$_____		____	$_____	
____	$_____		____	$_____		____	$_____	
____	$_____		____	$_____		____	$_____	
____	$_____		____	$_____		____	$_____	
	$_____			$_____			$_____	

Expense Item _____			Expense Item _____			Expense Item _____		
Line	Amount		Line	Amount		Line	Amount	
____	$_____		____	$_____		____	$_____	
____	$_____		____	$_____		____	$_____	
____	$_____		____	$_____		____	$_____	
____	$_____		____	$_____		____	$_____	
____	$_____		____	$_____		____	$_____	
	$_____			$_____			$_____	

Expense Item _____			Expense Item _____			Expense Item _____		
Line	Amount		Line	Amount		Line	Amount	
____	$_____		____	$_____		____	$_____	
____	$_____		____	$_____		____	$_____	
____	$_____		____	$_____		____	$_____	
____	$_____		____	$_____		____	$_____	
____	$_____		____	$_____		____	$_____	
	$_____			$_____			$_____	

Starting Day 15

Week 3

Diary for the Week

Today's Date: _____

Goal for the Week:

_____

_____

Payments due for the Week:

_____

_____

_____

Saving Ideas for the Week:

_____

_____

_____

Log – Thoughts, Reminders, and Accomplishments:

_____

_____

_____

_____

_____

_____

Weekly Expense Tracker Form

Line Item	Date	Description of Money Spent — For example: Purchased groceries, lunch at fast food restaurant, snacks, gasoline, oil change and gifts. Paid electric bill and etc.	Amount
1			$
2			$
3			$
4			$
5			$
6			$
7			$
8			$
9			$
10			$
11			$
12			$
13			$
14			$
15			$
16			$
17			$
18			$
19			$
20			$
Sub- Total 1			**$**

Go to next page and continue to log expenses for the week.

Weekly Expense Tracker Form

Line Item	Date	Description of Money Spent For example: Purchased groceries, lunch at fast food restaurant, snacks, gasoline, oil change and gifts. Paid electric bill and etc.	Amount
21			$
22			$
23			$
24			$
25			$
26			$
27			$
28			$
29			$
30			$
31			$
32			$
33			$
34			$
35			$
36			$
37			$
38			$
39			$
40			$
Sub-Total 2			$

Summary for the Week

Weekly Expense Tracker

    Sub-total 1 $_____

    Sub-total 2 $_____

    Total Expenses for the Week $_____

Check each box that summarizes your week's activities

- ☐ Used the Expense Tracker for the week
- ☐ Found ways to cut costs
- ☐ Paid bills on time
- ☐ Used coupons and discounts to save money
- ☐ Reduced use of credit cards
- ☐ Stayed on track with efforts to become debt-free
- ☐ Helped friends and family to start the Humpty's fitness plan

Notes – Weekly Activities and Achievements

_____
_____
_____
_____
_____

Books for Humpty financial fitness program can be ordered at
www.HumptyDumptyFinances.com

Expense Scratch Pad

(Week that Begins _____)

Expense Item _____			Expense Item _____			Expense Item _____		
Line	Amount		Line	Amount		Line	Amount	
___	$ _____		___	$ _____		___	$ _____	
___	$ _____		___	$ _____		___	$ _____	
___	$ _____		___	$ _____		___	$ _____	
___	$ _____		___	$ _____		___	$ _____	
___	$ _____		___	$ _____		___	$ _____	
	$ _____			$ _____			$ _____	

Expense Item _____			Expense Item _____			Expense Item _____		
Line	Amount		Line	Amount		Line	Amount	
___	$ _____		___	$ _____		___	$ _____	
___	$ _____		___	$ _____		___	$ _____	
___	$ _____		___	$ _____		___	$ _____	
___	$ _____		___	$ _____		___	$ _____	
___	$ _____		___	$ _____		___	$ _____	
	$ _____			$ _____			$ _____	

Expense Item _____			Expense Item _____			Expense Item _____		
Line	Amount		Line	Amount		Line	Amount	
___	$ _____		___	$ _____		___	$ _____	
___	$ _____		___	$ _____		___	$ _____	
___	$ _____		___	$ _____		___	$ _____	
___	$ _____		___	$ _____		___	$ _____	
___	$ _____		___	$ _____		___	$ _____	
	$ _____			$ _____			$ _____	

Starting Day 22

Week 4

Diary for the Week

Today's Date: _____

Goal for the Week:

_____
_____

Payments due for the Week:

_____
_____
_____

Saving Ideas for the Week:

_____
_____
_____

Log – Thoughts, Reminders, and Accomplishments:

_____
_____
_____
_____
_____
_____

Weekly Expense Tracker Form

Line Item	Date	Description of Money Spent — For example: Purchased groceries, lunch at fast food restaurant, snacks, gasoline, oil change and gifts. Paid electric bill and etc.	Amount
1			$
2			$
3			$
4			$
5			$
6			$
7			$
8			$
9			$
10			$
11			$
12			$
13			$
14			$
15			$
16			$
17			$
18			$
19			$
20			$
Sub-Total 1			$

Go to next page and continue to log expenses for the week.

Weekly Expense Tracker Form

Line Item	Date	Description of Money Spent For example: Purchased groceries, lunch at fast food restaurant, snacks, gasoline, oil change and gifts. Paid electric bill and etc.	Amount
21			$
22			$
23			$
24			$
25			$
26			$
27			$
28			$
29			$
30			$
31			$
32			$
33			$
34			$
35			$
36			$
37			$
38			$
39			$
40			$
Sub- Total 2			$

Summary for the Week

Weekly Expense Tracker

    Sub-total 1 $_____

    Sub-total 2 $_____

    Total Expenses for the Week $_____

Check each box that summarizes your week's activities

- ☐ Used the Expense Tracker for the week
- ☐ Found ways to cut costs
- ☐ Paid bills on time
- ☐ Used coupons and discounts to save money
- ☐ Reduced use of credit cards
- ☐ Stayed on track with efforts to become debt-free
- ☐ Helped friends and family to start the Humpty's fitness plan

Notes – Weekly Activities and Achievements

_____
_____
_____
_____
_____

Books for Humpty financial fitness program can be ordered at
www.HumptyDumptyFinances.com

Expense Scratch Pad

(Week that Begins _____)

Expense Item _____			Expense Item _____			Expense Item _____		
Line	Amount		Line	Amount		Line	Amount	
____	$ _____		____	$ _____		____	$ _____	
____	$ _____		____	$ _____		____	$ _____	
____	$ _____		____	$ _____		____	$ _____	
____	$ _____		____	$ _____		____	$ _____	
____	$ _____		____	$ _____		____	$ _____	
	$ _____			$ _____			$ _____	

Expense Item _____			Expense Item _____			Expense Item _____		
Line	Amount		Line	Amount		Line	Amount	
____	$ _____		____	$ _____		____	$ _____	
____	$ _____		____	$ _____		____	$ _____	
____	$ _____		____	$ _____		____	$ _____	
____	$ _____		____	$ _____		____	$ _____	
____	$ _____		____	$ _____		____	$ _____	
	$ _____			$ _____			$ _____	

Expense Item _____			Expense Item _____			Expense Item _____		
Line	Amount		Line	Amount		Line	Amount	
____	$ _____		____	$ _____		____	$ _____	
____	$ _____		____	$ _____		____	$ _____	
____	$ _____		____	$ _____		____	$ _____	
____	$ _____		____	$ _____		____	$ _____	
____	$ _____		____	$ _____		____	$ _____	
	$ _____			$ _____			$ _____	

Budget Months 1, 2 and 3
(Monthly Budgeting)

Month One

Monthly Budget & Actual

Month and Year _____   Page 1 of 2

Line Items	Budget	Actual	Variance
Gross Monthly Income	$	$	$
Contributions			
Church Tithes	$	$	$
Offerings/Charity	$	$	$
Total Contributions	$	$	$
Taxes			
Federal	$	$	$
State	$	$	$
Social Security & Medicare	$	$	$
Total Taxes	$	$	$
Savings & Investments			
Payroll Deductions (401k)	$	$	$
Savings	$	$	$
Mutual Funds	$	$	$
Total Savings & Investments	$	$	$
Liabilities			
Rent or Mortgage	$	$	$
Automobile	$	$	$
Credit Cards & Other Debts	$	$	$
Total Liabilities	$	$	$
Transportation			
Gas	$	$	$
Maintenance & Repairs	$	$	$
Car Tag & Fees	$	$	$
Total Transportation	$	$	$

Budget continues onto the next page.

Month one continued...

Monthly Budget & Actual

Month and Year _____

Line Items	Budget	Actual	Variance
Insurance			
Life, Health & Disability Ins.	$	$	$
Auto Insurance	$	$	$
Home Owner Insurance	$	$	$
Total Insurance	$	$	$
Household Expenses			
Food	$	$	$
Clothing	$	$	$
Doctor (including eye care)	$	$	$
Personal Care	$	$	$
Gas & Electricity	$	$	$
Maintenance & Repair	$	$	$
Home Furnishing	$	$	$
Phone & Internet Services	$	$	$
Water & Garbage Pick-up	$	$	$
Entertainment & Cable	$	$	$
Education, Books & Magazine	$	$	$
School Tuition and Other	$	$	$
Vacation & Travel	$	$	$
Gifts & Allowance	$	$	$
Other	$	$	$
Total Household Expenses	$	$	$
Total Monthly Expenses	$	$	$
Remaining Funds Allocate to Debt	$	$	$

Month Two

Monthly Budget & Actual

Month and Year _____   Page 1 of 2

Line Items	Budget	Actual	Variance
Gross Monthly Income	$	$	$
Contributions			
Church Tithes	$	$	$
Offerings/Charity	$	$	$
Total Contributions	$	$	$
Taxes			
Federal	$	$	$
State	$	$	$
Social Security & Medicare	$	$	$
Total Taxes	$	$	$
Savings & Investments			
Payroll Deductions (401k)	$	$	$
Savings	$	$	$
Mutual Funds	$	$	$
Total Savings & Investments	$	$	$
Liabilities			
Rent or Mortgage	$	$	$
Automobile	$	$	$
Credit Cards & Other Debts	$	$	$
Total Liabilities	$	$	$
Transportation			
Gas	$	$	$
Maintenance & Repairs	$	$	$
Car Tag & Fees	$	$	$
Total Transportation	$	$	$

Budget continues onto the next page.

Month two continued...

Monthly Budget & Actual

Month and Year _____   Page 2 of 2

Line Items	Budget	Actual	Variance
Insurance			
Life, Health & Disability Ins.	$	$	$
Auto Insurance	$	$	$
Home Owner Insurance	$	$	$
Total Insurance	$	$	$
Household Expenses			
Food	$	$	$
Clothing	$	$	$
Doctor (including eye care)	$	$	$
Personal Care	$	$	$
Gas & Electricity	$	$	$
Maintenance & Repair	$	$	$
Home Furnishing	$	$	$
Phone & Internet Services	$	$	$
Water & Garbage Pick-up	$	$	$
Entertainment & Cable	$	$	$
Education, Books & Magazine	$	$	$
School Tuition and Other	$	$	$
Vacation & Travel	$	$	$
Gifts & Allowance	$	$	$
Other	$	$	$
Total Household Expenses	$	$	$
Total Monthly Expenses	$	$	$
Remaining Funds Allocate to Debt	$	$	$

Month Three

Monthly Budget & Actual

Month and Year _____   Page 1 of 2

Line Items	Budget	Actual	Variance
Gross Monthly Income	$	$	$
Contributions			
Church Tithes	$	$	$
Offerings/Charity	$	$	$
Total Contributions	$	$	$
Taxes			
Federal	$	$	$
State	$	$	$
Social Security & Medicare	$	$	$
Total Taxes	$	$	$
Savings & Investments			
Payroll Deductions (401k)	$	$	$
Savings	$	$	$
Mutual Funds	$	$	$
Total Savings & Investments	$	$	$
Liabilities			
Rent or Mortgage	$	$	$
Automobile	$	$	$
Credit Cards & Other Debts	$	$	$
Total Liabilities	$	$	$
Transportation			
Gas	$	$	$
Maintenance & Repairs	$	$	$
Car Tag & Fees	$	$	$
Total Transportation	$	$	$

Budget continues onto the next page.

Month three continued...

Monthly Budget & Actual

Month and Year _____   Page 2 of 2

Line Items	Budget	Actual	Variance
Insurance			
Life, Health & Disability Ins.	$	$	$
Auto Insurance	$	$	$
Home Owner Insurance	$	$	$
Total Insurance	$	$	$
Household Expenses			
Food	$	$	$
Clothing	$	$	$
Doctor (including eye care)	$	$	$
Personal Care	$	$	$
Gas & Electricity	$	$	$
Maintenance & Repair	$	$	$
Home Furnishing	$	$	$
Phone & Internet Services	$	$	$
Water & Garbage Pick-up	$	$	$
Entertainment & Cable	$	$	$
Education, Books & Magazine	$	$	$
School Tuition and Other	$	$	$
Vacation & Travel	$	$	$
Gifts & Allowance	$	$	$
Other	$	$	$
Total Household Expenses	$	$	$
Total Monthly Expenses	$	$	$
Remaining Funds Allocate to Debt	$	$	$

Stephon Lee

ACKNOWLEDGEMENTS

I have a lot to be thankful for. First and far most, I give honor to God. I thank God for inspiration, strength and energy to complete this book. I am thankful to the many that have inspired and assisted me. I appreciate my pastor, Bishop William L. Sheals, for his many Spirit-filled sermons and encouragement. I thank my family and friends who have been there with a listening ear. I am grateful to people like Cassandra Watts, Winston Lee, Lyneice Hunter, John Mansfield, Hollis William, Lawrence Martin, Douglas Prather and Faithel Dubois who have taken time to review the book and provide their suggestions. I appreciate my son, Daniel, who shared many of his thoughts and ideas with me. I thank my wife, Joyce, for being there. I thank Bob Adkins, Tony Mitchell and Sharron Kelly for sharing their industry knowledge and insight. I appreciate Michael Jones for his God given wisdom. I value Doug Craig for his creative thoughts. I appreciate Stephanie and Richard for their administrative support.

ABOUT THE AUTHOR

Stephon Lee is an author, entrepreneur and business consultant that speaks on the topic of finances.

He is a certified lean six sigma black belt by the Georgia Institute of Technology and business consultant, who consults major companies on ways to increase productivity, reduce costs and make ongoing process improvements.

Stephon has written his first book titled, "Humpty Dumpty Finances" to give companies a simple tool to help their employees to be more financially fit. The book is an easy road map to guide individuals to better financial success.

In 2005, he founded Budget Your Dream Incorporated to provide innovative software solutions to banking institutions and financial counseling agencies; by which he was able to successfully help individuals develop financial skills, reduce debts, sustain home-ownership and build wealth.

Stephon is currently writing his second book titled "Living

Debt Free for Kingdom Building" and will continue to share his knowledge to inspire and help many more to overcome challenges, grow wealth and achieve greater financial success.